P9-DOD-170

The Library of Author Biographies™

Christopher Paul Curtis

The Library of Author Biographies™

CHRISTOPHER PAUL CURTIS

Judy Levin

rosen central™

The Rosen Publishing Group, Inc., New York

NEW HANOVER COUNTY
PUBLIC LIBRARY
201 CHESTNUT STREET
WILMINGTON, NC 28401

For Laura

Published in 2006 by The Rosen Publishing Group, Inc.
29 East 21st Street, New York, NY 10010

Copyright © 2006 by The Rosen Publishing Group, Inc.

First Edition

All rights reserved. No part of this book may be reproduced in any form without permission in writing from the publisher, except by a reviewer.

Library of Congress Cataloging-in-Publication Data

Levin, Judy, 1978–
Christopher Paul Curtis / Judy Levin.—1st ed.
p. cm.—(The library of author biographies)
Includes bibliographical references and index.
ISBN 1-4042-0458-X (lib. bdg.)
ISBN 1-4042-0647-7 (pbk. bdg.)
1. Curtis, Christopher Paul. 2. Authors, American—20th century—Biography. 3. African American authors—Biography. 4. Young adult fiction—Authorship.
I. Title. II. Series.
PS3553.U6944Z76 2005
813'.54—dc22

2005001368

Manufactured in the United States of America

From Eighth Book of Juniors Authors and Illustrators, Copyright © 2000, edit by Connie C. Rockman. Reprinted with permission of The H. W. Wilson Company.

Quotes from Johnson, Nancy J., & Giorgis, Cyndi. (Dec. 2000/Jan. 2001). 2000 Newbery Medal winner: A conversation with Christopher Paul Curtis. The Reading Teacher, 54(4), 424–428. Reprinted with permission of the International Reading Association.

Text © 2000 by Wendy Lamb. The Horn Book Magazine, July/August 2000. Reprinted by permission of The Horn Book, Inc., Boston, MA, www.hbook.com.

From: Teri Lesesne and Christopher Paul Curtis, "Writing the Stories Brewing Inside of Us," Reprinted with permission from Teacher Librarian: The Journal for School Library Professionals, Vol. 27(4), p. 60.

From "Good Conversations: A Talk with Christopher Paul Curtis," Tim Podell Productions, P.O. Box 244 Scarborough, NY 10510, 1-800-642-4181, www.goodconversations.com. Reproduced with permission.

Table of Contents

Introduction: Factory Worker Becomes Novelist

"Humor gives you strength," says Christopher Paul Curtis. "It allows you to build up antibodies to all the horrible things in the world."[1]

Curtis's books are full of humor and "horrible things," too. *The Watsons Go to Birmingham—1963* is a hilariously funny tale, yet it ends with the 1963 Birmingham church bombing that killed four African American girls. Curtis's ability to inspire laughter and provoke thought have made him an award-winning, best-selling author starting with his first book—and it changed his life.

After *The Watsons Go to Birmingham—1963* was published, Curtis became famous.

His second book, *Bud, Not Buddy*, won the 2000 Newbery Medal as the best American children's book published the previous year, and it received the Coretta Scott King Award for the best book published by an African American writer. That made *Bud* the first book to win both awards in the same year and Curtis the first African American man to win the Newbery Medal since the award was received in 1977 by Mildred D. Taylor for *Roll of Thunder, Hear My Cry*.

Readers enjoy Curtis's own story, too. The way the newspapers tell it, Curtis was a factory worker who became a best-selling writer. That's almost true. He had worked for thirteen years on the assembly line in an auto plant, hanging eighty-pound (thirty-six-kilogram) doors on Buicks and hating every minute of it. Curtis quit that job to take other work that he hated nearly as much, like unloading trucks in a warehouse. The success of his first book meant that, in his early forties, he could finally stop doing jobs that he hated and write full time—a job he loves. It was a dream come true, and Curtis won't let anyone forget that it was his wife, Kaysandra, and her belief in his talent that helped make that dream a reality. He notes: "She had more faith in my ability to write than I did."[2]

In addition to writing *The Watsons* and *Bud*, Curtis has written *Bucking the Sarge*. These three books are set in different time periods. In *Bucking the Sarge,* his narrator is a little older (aged fifteen compared to ten), but the books have much in common. All three are set in Flint, Michigan, where Curtis grew up. Each are filled with wacky humor that acts as an "antibody" against the horrible things the main character encounters. All three have first-person narrators who tell their story in their own words. In each book, Curtis writes about African American communities in which there are few white characters or references to white people. And yet his books are enjoyed by children and adults of all cultures.

Curtis says that part of his success came because he is writing to fill a void: there are too few books written for middle-grade or young-adult African American readers. He is still surprised, he says, when he attends author conferences and sees how few writers of color there are. He hopes that will change in the future. When he was a boy, he was a good reader, yet after he wrote his books, children would ask him what books he had loved when he was young. The question made him realize there had been too few books written by, for, or about African Americans.

Curtis does not believe that black kids should only read about black kids. To love literature, he says, you have to start by finding those books that touch your heart. Curtis understands what it means to want to read about familiar experiences because when he was a boy he could not find books that seemed to be about him. At the same time, he is delighted when white or Asian readers, as well as blacks, read his books and jokingly ask him, "Were you in my closet? That's just like my family."[3]

Curtis's books include references to historical events and tragedies, yet they are fun to read—even his bad guys are funny. Plus, much of what his characters experience is familiar to everyone. His characters tease one another or worry about being teased. They try to figure out what to do when other people, such as a brother or a bully, behave in confusing or scary ways. They worry about monsters. They want to know there is someone who loves them and a place where they belong. They also worry that the people they love can die. Regardless of the characters' ages or the eras they live in, we understand them and their problems because we share the same experiences. Despite all those serious subjects, Curtis finds a way to make us laugh—not bad for a man who published his first book at forty-two years of age.

1 Meet the Flintstones

Christopher Paul Curtis was born on May 10, 1953, in Flint, Michigan. It's Luther, the fifteen-year-old narrator of *Bucking the Sarge,* who calls the city's residents "Flintstones." Curtis says he doesn't know why "the stories keep going to Flint . . . I don't understand the attraction, but if they want to keep going to Flint, that's where they'll go."[1]

Although none of Curtis's novels is autobiographical, his family was much like the Watsons. There were five Curtis children, not three—Christopher was the second. But like the Watsons, the Curtis children were raised in a house filled with love and discipline. Curtis also grew up during the era of the Watsons; like

Kenny Watson, Curtis was ten years old in 1963. When readers ask him which of his characters he resembles most, he jokes that he likes to think he was sensitive like Kenny. However, Curtis's brother David, who's four years younger than he is, says that Byron is his brother's self-portrait. Like Byron, Curtis dropped flaming paper Nazi paratroopers into the toilet and was caught by his mother, threatened with having his finger burned, and rescued by his younger sister, Cydney. Her picture is on the cover of *The Watsons*, as is a picture of Curtis's parents.

Curtis's mother, Leslie Lewis Curtis, was tough and protective like Mrs. Watson, but unlike the character, she graduated from Michigan State University. Although she stayed home to raise her children, as the majority of women did in the 1950s and 1960s, she later taught African American history. Curtis's father, Herman E. Curtis Jr., worked as a chiropodist (foot doctor) but had difficulty making enough money to support his family. His patients were often too poor to pay him, so in 1953 he went to work in one of the city's car factories, Flint Fisher Body Number One. In those days, working at a car plant was a secure way to make a high salary.

Curtis had a happy childhood. His parents had strict rules about doing chores and schoolwork, always treating people with respect, and going to bed early. "Six thirty! There we would be, bright sunlight outside, and all the Curtises were lying in their beds."[2] Curtis did not always like his parents' rules, yet they gave him a sense of security. "We knew the rules we had to follow and we knew what we had to do and what was expected of us."[3]

There was also a great deal of teasing, especially when Grandpa Earl "Lefty" Lewis was around. He told young Curtis about the old superstition that if you could put salt on a bird's tail you could catch it. Then Grandpa laughed heartily while Curtis tore around the yard with the saltshaker. The future author's father and other grandfather were teases, too, and it rubbed off on Curtis.

Members of the Curtis family were talented, intelligent, and enterprising. His father's father, Herman Curtis Sr., had studied violin at the Indiana Conservatory of Music. Although it was a place where musicians trained to play classical music, the senior Curtis—like the bandleader in *Bud, Not Buddy*—played all kinds of music from jazz to polka. Herman E. Curtis and the Dusky Devastators of the Depression was one of his bands. He also painted cars and trucks, drove a boat, and did other odd jobs. It was hard to earn a living during the Great Depression. The young Curtis inherited his grandfather's love of music. Though he is not a musician himself, he admits that music has always been important in his life (he often plays his collection of thousands of old LP records) and in his books.

Curtis's other grandfather, Earl Lewis, was a "red cap"—he loaded luggage onto trains. Although this might not seem as glamorous as being a musician, the railroad was an important source of jobs for black men in the early twentieth century. Lewis earned so much money in tips that his wife had to sew extra-heavy pockets in his pants so the weight of the coins would not tear holes in his trousers.

The railroad system eventually became important to the civil rights movement. Railroad porters—the men who worked on the trains helping passengers—formed the first black labor union. It was called the Brotherhood of Sleeping Car Porters. Before there was a national civil rights movement, there was a national labor movement, showing how ordinary people could work together to demand their rights. They were, as old Mr. Stockard says in *Bucking the Sarge*, "revolutionaries in [their] time."[4]

Lewis had earned his nickname, "Lefty," as a left-handed pitcher in the Negro Leagues. These baseball leagues were created because blacks were not allowed to play major league ball during the first half of the twentieth century. Although Lewis had played mostly in the Negro League minors, he pitched a couple of games against pitcher Leroy "Satchel" Paige, among the most famous players in the Negro Leagues. He lost, but everyone lost to Satchel Paige.

The Curtis children sometimes felt that their mother was too protective of them. It's a kind of protectiveness that Christopher Paul Curtis admitted he never understood until he had kids of his own. Curtis remembered his parents' restrictions as annoying—like when his mother refused to let the family go from door-to-door throughout the neighborhood during Halloween. She was convinced that everyone living in Flint was a potential poisoner. There was no way that she was going to let her children go outside to collect apples that might have razor blades hidden in them or candy bars that might be full of poison.

At the time Curtis was growing up, his mother was not the only parent who worried about such things, but Mrs. Curtis had an unusual solution to the problem. In the Curtis household, children put on their Halloween costumes to go trick-or-treating inside the house. They would knock on a bedroom door, their mother would put some candy in their bags, and then she would go to the next room and do the same thing. By the time they were knocking on the bathroom door for treats, they had become so bored with the activity that they were ready to quit.

Civil Rights

At just about five or six years of age, Curtis became aware of racism. He became aware that there were restaurants in Michigan that would not employ blacks. When his family joined the civil rights movement and went to picket these restaurants, he was spit on and ridiculed. Subjecting their children to such actions might seem like an odd thing for parents to do, but the Curtises believed that their children needed to understand the dangers that blacks often faced in the United States. The children also learned about segregation in the South. (The separate water fountains for blacks and whites that Mr. Watson refers to in *The Watsons Go to Birmingham—1963* are an example of segregation). They knew that some blacks were lynched in the South. Obviously, the North had not solved its race problems either, or the Curtis family would not be picketing restaurants. However, Curtis grew up with a fear of the South. The South was confusing to him: many of the families he knew that had come north or west from the South had come for jobs and to escape violence. Many were homesick, as Mrs. Watson is. Yet, shortly after Curtis was born, some counties in the South shut down public schools rather than integrate white and black students. This violated the 1954 U.S. Supreme Court ruling that public schools could no longer be segregated.

That Supreme Court decision, *Brown v. Board of Education*, helped spark the modern civil rights movement. In 1896, a Supreme Court decision had said that "separate but equal" facilities were constitutional. This ruling had paved the way for fifty-eight years of legally segregated schools, restaurants, movie theaters, public bathrooms, cemeteries, buses, trains, phone booths, and other public facilities in the South. Then, in December 1954, a young African American woman, Rosa Parks, was arrested for refusing to give up her seat to a white man on a Montgomery, Alabama, bus. For more than a year, the black citizens of Montgomery boycotted the transportation system, an action that launched more than ten years of peaceful civil rights protests, like the ones in which the Curtises participated. The movement also brought the young Baptist minister Martin Luther King Jr. to national attention.

Christopher Paul Curtis was ten years old when he watched police in Birmingham, Alabama, use fire hoses and attack dogs on protesters on the television news. The protesters, some as young as six years old, were among the 250,000 people who went to Washington, D.C., to hear King give his "I have a dream" speech. At the same time, four white men blew up the Sixteenth Street Baptist Church in Birmingham during Sunday school, killing four girls and maiming many other children and adults.

Like the Watson kids, the Curtis children grew up in an all-black community in the North. They had a few white teachers and saw white people on television, but their neighbors, store owners, and doctors—all the adults and children they saw regularly—were black. Martin Luther King Jr. and Rosa Parks, who grew up in the segregated South, had white neighbors and white friends. In the North, there were fewer segregation laws, yet neighborhoods were often entirely segregated. The Curtis family and other people involved in the civil rights movement did not want blacks banned from jobs or neighborhoods. There was a lot of pride in the community.

When Curtis's editor, Wendy Lamb, was working on *The Watsons*, she asked Curtis what the character Kenny thought of white people. She wondered if readers would react to the fact that there were no white people in the book. Curtis said no, Kenny did not often think about white people. Curtis was answering from his own memories of being a boy in Flint in the 1960s.

Education

Although African Americans are a minority in the United States, they are plentiful in Curtis's books. Their culture shows in his language. A "child" means a black child. If a character is white, then that is noted. It is the opposite treatment of characters found in most young adult books. It seems like a small detail, but it's important—and it's one reason black readers can be at home with Curtis's books.

Like Kenny in *The Watsons*, Christopher Curtis was a good reader. His parents read thousands of books. "They saw us reading continuously,"[5] says Mrs. Curtis, and if the children were reading, they were allowed to stay up past their bedtimes. Curtis's father took the kids to the library on Saturdays. Curtis remembers how proud he was the first day his father said Curtis was ready to go to the adults' sections instead of the kids' department. He borrowed spy stories from his dad, and his parents bought the *World Book Encyclopedia* and other reference books, though they could not really afford them. Curtis read superhero comic books with his cousin. He read all the magazines in his house—*Time, Newsweek, Life, Sports Illustrated*—and enjoyed the wacky humor of *Mad* magazine. However, there weren't specific books that touched his heart because none he read was about kids like him. His favorite book became *To Kill a Mockingbird* by Harper Lee. It detailed events surrounding the legal defense of a black man who had been falsely charged with the rape of a white woman. Generally, it was not until Curtis was an adult that he began to find books that he truly loved.

Reading, writing, and education were important in the Curtis home, and not just for children. One day when Curtis was ten years old, he opened the front door to find a group of strange men. Suddenly, he remembered the family rule about not opening the door without a parent's permission. Immediately, his imaginative mind jumped to conclusions. He thought the men were burglars. The five men at the door were actually from the factory where his father worked, and they had come to the house for math lessons. Curtis's dad would teach them for months until they could pass a test at the factory and be promoted to higher-paying jobs.

Curtis was always a good writer, but remembers that when he was in school, his teachers valued correctness more than creativity. When he was young, he threatened to write a novel someday, and his sister Cydney said she thought he would be a great author because he told such good stories. Still, even in this book-loving family, nobody thought of writing as a way to earn a living. Curtis instead thought he might grow up to be an athlete, a doctor, or a lawyer.

2 The Jungle

After Christopher Paul Curtis graduated from high school in 1971, he was accepted into the University of Michigan. Before he began, however, he worked in a theater company. Curtis traveled to Lansing, Michigan, for rehearsals at the Suitcase Theater and toured with the company throughout the United States, Canada, and Europe. He and his sisters had acted in local theater groups when he was growing up, something his mother encouraged.

Curtis was a natural performer. In ninth grade, as he was about to lose the election for student council vice president, he got up to make his why-you-should-vote-for-me speech but instead sang a parody of the then-popular song "Sunny." Everyone stood up and cheered, and he won the race. Still, by the time he returned from the European tour, he realized that his personality was much different from many of the theater students he later encountered. Curtis felt that he didn't fit in. Later, when he started college, he majored in political science.

As it turned out, Curtis did not enjoy college. He frequently skipped classes and failed many of his courses. Within a short time, he decided to work in Flint, in Flint Fisher Body Number One, where his father worked and where he himself once had a summer job. His mother had been afraid he would do this. Nine dollars an hour was a lot of money in 1972. Therefore, it was easy to say yes to what that money could buy instead of continuing college and maybe not being able to earn a higher salary at the end of four years. After all, his father had given up his profession to work at the factory. Curtis bought a brand-new car (a yellow Camaro) and got his own apartment. Instead of a five-dollar-a-week allowance, he was making hundreds of dollars each week. Many people were supporting whole families on what he was earning.

General Motors

Each of Curtis's novels is set in a different era, and each reflects a different phase of the rise and decline of the American auto industry. In the early days of the industry, General Motors was founded in Flint in 1908. As the industry expanded, the city attracted blacks from the South who were looking for work. During the 1910s, insects, namely boll weevils, began destroying cotton crops, the mainstay of the Southern economy and the source of jobs for many black families. At the time, millions of blacks left the South in search of jobs and, if not racial equality, at least the right to vote and to go to integrated movie theaters.

In 1936 and 1937, Flint was the site of one of the most significant labor strikes of the twentieth century. In the factory where Curtis and his father would later be employed, workers not only went on strike, but they sat down on the job so that the factory owners could not replace them. Factory owners asked the government to bring in the National Guard to help them remove the strikers. After the soldiers arrived, the streets of Flint were full of tanks, and an agreement was reached moments before the troops launched a full-scale attack on the workers.

Set in 1936 during the Great Depression, *Bud, Not Buddy* recalls the era when labor unions were organized in the auto factories. In the book, Lefty Lewis, a porter who belonged to the Brotherhood of Sleeping Car Porters (BSCP) union, rescues Bud in the middle of the night during his long walk from Flint to Grand Rapids, Michigan. Although its significance was at the time unknown to Bud, the BSCP was the first African American labor union in the United States and the first to win a collective bargaining agreement with the Pullman Rail Car Company. Bud is running away, and after Lewis picks him up, his car is stopped by police. However, the cops do not find the stash of labor organization fliers under Bud's seat. Lewis explains that the leaflets are dangerous and that they had to be printed in Flint because no one in Grand Rapids would print them. At the time, Bud does not understand that those fliers could have gotten Lewis killed.

The Watsons Go to Birmingham—1963, is, as the title says, set in 1963—a time when the factories were providing secure jobs for anyone with a high school diploma. That was still true when Curtis began working at the plant in 1972. But by the time of Curtis's third book, *Bucking the Sarge*, the American auto industry had fallen on hard times. The auto factories of Flint were no longer providing jobs, and no other industries had taken their place in the city's economy. As a result, there was a great deal of poverty in Flint and little hope for an improved economy in the region. In *Bucking the Sarge*, Luther's best friend Sparky is not alone in thinking that the only thing to do in Flint is to scam the welfare system or leave Flint forever. To Sparky, the city has become a dead end.

For Curtis, the car factory was a different kind of dead end. He worked on an assembly line, attaching 80-pound (36 kg) doors to Buicks, over and over again. It wasn't that the work was hard, because Curtis is a big man—6 feet 2 inches (1.9 meters) tall and about 180 pounds (81.7 kg), with broad shoulders. But it was noisy, hot, mind-numbing, and boring. Sheets of steel that would eventually become Buicks screamed as they were torn, bent, and melted by 4-feet-long (1.2 m) welding guns. The air was smoky. Curtis would later write:

> [When] . . . you hear the KERCHUNKA-KERCUNKA-KERCHUNKA sound of the welders pounding their guns into the steel sounding like the largest elephant ever born is crashing through the bushes and stomping the hell out of anything in the way or sounding like drums pounding out some message that you don't get, then you can understand how the name Jungle fits so well.[1]

Around 1977 Curtis met nursing student Kaysandra Sookram at a Flint versus Hamilton, Ontario, basketball game in Canada. Born in

Trinidad, Sookram was smart, beautiful, and hardworking—and she liked basketball. Sookram and Curtis began to carry out their courtship by mail when the long-distance phone calls became too expensive. At that time, Sookram realized that her fiance was a talented writer. Their first child, Steven, was born in 1978. Their daughter, Cydney, named for Curtis's sister, wouldn't come along until 1992. Kaysandra Curtis worked as a nurse while her husband continued to work—and loathe—his factory job.

Thirty Minutes at a Time

Curtis and a coworker at the factory made a deal: instead of putting on every other door hour after hour, each one would work twice as hard for a half hour and put on thirty doors, and then have a half hour off while the other did the same. That gave each of them thirty minutes of every hour as a break, and Curtis used his time to write. Part of the time, he wrote about how much he hated his job.

Reading helped. At the time, he was attending classes part-time at the university, and a course in black literature introduced him to books by Zora Neale Hurston, Alice Walker, and—one of his favorite writers—Toni Morrison. He had finally found literature that touched his heart—although he also enjoyed a wide range of novelists, including Kurt Vonnegut and 1950s crime writer Jim Thompson.

Writing helped in a different way. As a boy, Curtis had written stories based on the 1960s television series *The Man from U.N.C.L.E.* The show was full of spies and starred a cool, sarcastic hero named Napoleon Solo. Later Curtis tried to write spy stories like the ones he'd borrowed from his father. Curtis's spy worked in a bank, and had a key to the water-cooler that allowed him to escape to his "spy" room. Curtis thought his childhood stories were terrible.

Then he wrote about a friend of his who had an abusive father. The dad would do things like put his kids into the car and drive onto a frozen lake, spinning the car around while the kids screamed and cried, sure that they would crash through the ice and drown. Curtis didn't like how any of these stories turned out either. Still, these early failures helped him find his way as a writer. The abusive father was horrible, and yet, there's a funny weirdness about a grown man whipping his car around a frozen lake surrounded by startled ice fisherman. Curtis's character was an abusive dad with a creative streak. That combination of cruelty and absurdity began to resemble what would later become a typical character in a

Christopher Curtis novel. Most important, Curtis began to realize how important writing was for him. It provided an oasis of quiet in his mind. The writing process was a "refuge."[2] And having only half an hour at a time to write was good discipline.

Yet when Curtis quit his job in 1985, it wasn't because of his writing. He just couldn't stand to work at the factory any longer. When he tried to sleep at night, he hallucinated that his bed was moving across the floor at just the speed that the conveyer belt carried the cars. To help make ends meet, Curtis did odd jobs like mowing lawns and working as a maintenance man. He was also the campaign manager for a Michigan politician in 1988—just long enough to discover that he hated politics. Then the family moved across the border to Canada in 1985, which made things easier for Kaysandra Curtis, whose license to practice nursing was Canadian. At the same time, Curtis continued doing odd jobs he disliked, such as loading trucks in a warehouse.

3 *The Watsons* Changes Everything

In 1993, everything started to change for Christopher Paul Curtis. He was still attending the University of Michigan that year and won the Avery Hopwood Prize for an essay he wrote about his decision to leave his factory job. His winning essay focused on the day that he knew he needed to leave. In it he describes the factory as a jungle, and the day when, after thirteen years, he made that final walk out the door. "I felt," he wrote, that "every dream, every hope, every talent I ever had was being melted away by the numbing horror, the endless repetition, the daily grind of that factory."[1] In the essay, a coworker rescues him as he stands frozen, "amazed that [he could be] so unhappy and wasn't crying." His friend helps him to his car and suggests he take a day off: "Some of the time it's just too much, isn't it?"[2]

The prize was the first public recognition that Curtis was a good writer, but Kaysandra Curtis had been telling him that for years. She wanted him to take a year off work to write full-time. Since she worked as a nurse in an intensive care unit, she made enough money to support the family. Also, she was tired of seeing her husband so miserable. She suggested he "better hurry up and start doing something constructive with his life or else start looking for a new place to live."[3] But mostly she just believed in him. Later that year when Curtis was on stage accepting two Jules Hopwood Prizes—one for his essay and another for an early draft of *The Watsons Go to Birmingham—1963*—Kaysandra sat in the audience talking to the mother of another prize-winner. The woman later told Curtis, "You know, with a wife like that you don't have any choice but to be a success as a writer."[4]

The story that would become *The Watsons* was one he had thought about for a few years, ever since he drove from Windsor, Ontario, to Florida to visit Kaysandra's sister. One of the few things Curtis had liked about his factory job was listening to the workers' conversations. Many were from the South and still had relatives there. They would talk about driving south, sometimes going twenty-four or even thirty-six hours without stopping. When his family drove down to Florida, Curtis wanted to see if he could make the trip nonstop. Like Mr. Watson, he didn't tell his wife what he had in mind. He did manage to drive twenty-four hours straight. However, he was so tired while driving through some mountain ranges and towns that he can't even remember them.

But when Curtis tried to write a novel about a family traveling to Florida, he ran into problems. First, he tried to have the thirteen-year-old character Byron pose as the story's narrator, but that didn't work: Byron was such a liar that he lied even to Curtis. The author instead relied on Kenny to tell the story. That helped. But then, when Curtis got his fictional family to Florida, he ran into a real problem: nothing much happened.

Curtis's year of writing full-time was wonderful, but also scary. Sometimes he was afraid of failure, afraid of wasting such a great chance. Still, Curtis has never believed in writer's block. When he gets stuck, he doesn't think that his creativity has gone or that all his ideas have faded. Instead, he believes that something has gone wrong with his story, and he has to figure out what that is. When he writes, he likes to have several projects going at once. That way, if he needs to put one aside, he can move on to something else in the meantime to clear his mind. Soon, with little effort, he'll figure out what the problem is with the other project and return to it.

Despite his anxiety, Curtis continued to work within the writing schedule he had created for himself. He got up at 5 AM to read what he wrote the day before and edit it. The early hour was not new to Curtis—his factory job had required him to start early, too. Now that he was his own boss, he could certainly maintain his rigorous schedule. After getting Cydney up and ready for school, Curtis would head over to the Windsor Public Library's children's section to write, longhand, on a yellow legal-sized pad. (Curtis's second book, *Bud, Not Buddy*, eventually required twenty-five yellow pads!) He liked to play basketball midday whenever possible, to let off tension. Then, every night, his son, Steven, typed up *The Watsons* for him. This was useful because Steven would tell his father if there was anything he didn't like, and why. Also, Curtis's typing was slow and full of errors.

Just as Curtis was trying to figure out what to do with *The Watsons*, Steven brought a poem home from school called "Ballad of Birmingham," written in 1965 by Dudley Randall. In it, a girl asks her mother if she can go downtown and take part in that day's protest, but the mother is afraid her daughter will be hurt. Lovingly the mother dresses the girl and sends her to church, where she expected she would be safe. When the mother hears an explosion and rushes to the church, she can find only her daughter's shoe.

All at once, Curtis realized that the Watsons were meant to go to Birmingham, Alabama, not Florida, and that the story should include the discovery of a shoe in the church rubble. Curtis wrote the last chapters of the book very quickly, in about a month. By the beginning of 1994, Curtis's book about an ordinary Flint family in 1963 was finished. The father works in the Buick plant and the mother takes care of the house and family. The narrator, ten-year-old Kenny, is a good student and has a lazy eye, so he gets teased a lot. He loves, admires, and worries about his older brother, Byron, a rebellious thirteen-year-old, who joins a gang. Byron sometimes takes money from his mom's purse, cuts school, and gets into fights.

The reader—and sometimes Kenny—can see that part of Byron's tough attitude is just a role he plays. There are a few exceptions, however, like when Byron gets his hair chemically straightened and dyed. After Byron's father shaves the boy's head, the family decides to take Byron down to Alabama to spend the summer with the strict grandmother who raised Mrs. Watson, far away from his troubled friends.

The beginning of *The Watsons* is incredibly funny. Still, Curtis flawlessly and carefully prepares his readers for the serious ending. At the beginning of the story, which begins during a cold winter in Flint, Michigan, death is just a joke. When Byron and his rough friend Buphead decide to toughen up Kenny by exaggerating the effects of a blizzard, Buphead makes blizzard noises: "Wooo! Look out! Blizzard a-comin'! Death around the corner! Look out!"[5] Then Byron spits a mouthful of snow at his brother.

Soon after, little sister Joella complains about how their Southern-born mom makes them wear too many clothes while outdoors and insists that they'll freeze to death if they don't. Joella is little, but she's no fool. She says that none of the other kids has to dress so warmly, and she doesn't see anyone lying around frozen to death. Next, Byron tells her a story about how some of the garbage trucks she sees are fakes. These trucks are really driving around, he claims, to pick up all of the people who have frozen to death. Kenny has his doubts, but the story is enough to keep Joella from complaining about being too hot. Early in the story, death is something to frighten children with, like a bogeyman. At the end of the book, the serious nature of death is finally realized. To Kenny, death is like a faceless monster. (Curtis borrowed this image of death from a book by the famous African American writer Zora Neale Hurston, author of many books including *Their Eyes Were Watching God*.) Throughout *The Watsons,* Curtis has written about death as if it were a false threat. Only at the book's conclusion does the reader understand the heartbreak and finality of the loss of life.

In Birmingham, the Watsons face Southern heat, their first outhouse, and their tiny, fierce grandmother. To Kenny's disgust, Byron takes one look at his grandmother and becomes miraculously obedient. When the children are forbidden to swim in a particularly inviting waterhole because of a dangerous whirlpool, Byron obeys. He tells Kenny that the "Wool Pooh" is Winnie-the-Pooh's evil twin brother. Because Kenny believes this to be another tale, just like his brother's story about the fake garbage trucks full of dead, frozen people, he ignores the warning. Drowning, Kenny sees what he imagines to be the figure of the Wool Pooh. He also sees a vision of his sister as an angel, telling him he must struggle to the surface one more time. Byron rescues him, then collapses. As Byron sobs on his brother, he shows he is not a tough guy at all. But the imaginary figure he sees while struggling—a symbol of death—has become real to Kenny.

On the following Sunday, there is a sound like thunder. The news spreads quickly that the church where Joella is attending Sunday school has been bombed. Slipping inside the church unnoticed, Kenny sees the bodies of two dead girls being carried out. Then he sees a shoe just like his sister's. He wrestles the shoe away from the Wool Pooh, but then flees terrified that death will come after him again. He is so sure that his sister has died that when she comes home, he doesn't believe it's really her. Joella yells at Kenny for scaring her, but says that he should know that she wasn't in the church. She claims that he had beckoned to her, and she ran after him. In the story, Joella is saved by a vision of her brother, as he had been saved by one of her.

Back in Flint, Kenny checks himself into the World-Famous Watson's Pet Hospital. It's the place behind the couch where sick pets are left to heal or die in a household that can't afford veterinary services. (When Curtis was a boy his family was also too poor to take the family pets to the local vet.)

Kenny believes he was a coward who left his sister behind in the church. He saw children killed by a racist hatred he cannot comprehend and one that his parents cannot explain to him. It is Byron who drags Kenny back to the land of the living, insisting that he did save his sister, since it was a vision of him that saved her. Byron also provides a better explanation of the church bombing than the adults have been able to offer. Their parents say that the people who bombed the church were "sick," but Byron says, "I think they just let hate eat them up and turn them into monsters."[6]

In the end, Kenny accepts his brother's promise that he will be OK. Yet he thinks Byron is wrong about the Wool Pooh—it was real. Even if Byron is right when he says there's no magic behind the couch, there is still a kind of magic in what Kenny has done and in the power that their tiny grandmother had when she hugged them upon their arrival in Birmingham. It's what Curtis believes is strong magic: the power of families. This is a theme that becomes important in all of Curtis's books.

Publication

Curtis believed that he'd created a good novel, but he had to find a publisher. He entered *The Watsons* in two competitions—one at Little, Brown (which turned it down) and one at Delacorte, which later became interested in Curtis's work. Delacorte held an annual competition for a first novel written for young adults. *The Watsons Go to Birmingham—1963* wasn't really for young adults, and when Curtis was writing it, he didn't think of it as a children's book either. It was just the story he wanted to tell, and the narrator was ten years old.

Many readers don't know what the "1963" in the title of the book represents until they get to the end. But Wendy Lamb, the editor in charge of the Delacorte writing competition, knew immediately. Covered with "gray fuzz from the innards of exploding jiffy [mailing] bags"[7] as she opened manuscripts for the contest, she made a special note of *The Watsons*. She was impressed that a first-time novelist would write about something so difficult and important. Then, when she read it, she was amazed that the book could be so funny when it was going to end very seriously.

Curtis's book didn't win the contest, however, because it wasn't written for children and because it was historical in nature, rather than contemporary fiction. But Delacorte asked to publish *The Watsons* anyway. The publisher even gave Curtis a contract for three more books, so they could keep publishing his work. Curtis began working with Wendy Lamb as his regular editor, a relationship they both enjoy, teasing and laughing with each other as they go through the hard work of revising a novel. "Working with him is like working with a brother—but without the punching,"[8] Lamb says. *The Watsons* required relatively little revision, but in a book for middle-grade readers, the whirlpool scene needed to be shortened and made less frightening.

The publishers also suggested a different epilogue for the book. Curtis wanted to include a statement made by a white Birmingham lawyer at the time of the 1963 church bombing. The man had said that every person who had ever ignored injustice to a black person was responsible for those girls' deaths. It was a courageous statement for that time and place. But, instead, Lamb wanted Curtis to explain a little about the civil rights movement and the racial injustice that had made the movement necessary. Curtis was glad to write the revision. Most of all, he wanted his books to be read and enjoyed, but he also hoped that his stories would encourage some readers to learn more about the struggle for civil rights. Curtis wants readers to see what Joella's death would have meant to the Watson family. Readers know the family so well that, decades after the bombing, they can feel at least a little of the horror and pain of what it meant to lose a child so violently. Readers also understand what it meant for Kenny to try to comprehend the hatred that caused the deaths.

Honors

Critics were as impressed with *The Watsons* as Wendy Lamb had been, and, like her, were startled and impressed by the contrast between the book's humor and its depiction of tragedy. Like first-grade teachers and movie critics, book reviewers rate work by using stars—the more stars, the better the work. *The Watsons* received a lot of stars.

By January 1996, Curtis had heard that his book was being considered for the Coretta Scott King Award. That award, first given in 1970 to honor Martin Luther King Jr.'s widow, is for the best book of the year by an African American children's author. The award is announced at the midwinter meeting of the American Library Association (ALA). The ALA also announces the Newbery Medal and Honor books. The Newbery Medal is the most prestigious honor that an American children's book can win. There was a possibility that the Newbery committee might also be considering *The Watsons*.

Curtis says he had heard (incorrectly) that winning writers would hear on Sunday night if they had won an award, although the awards are not announced officially until Monday morning:

> That Sunday evening in the Curtis household was horrible. The phone never rang. I even picked it up several times to make certain we had a dial tone. Finally at 11:00 PM I called it a night. Kay stayed up . . . The last thing I said to her as I went upstairs was, "Aww, who wants those old awards anyway?"[9]

The following morning, Curtis went to the Windsor Public Library to write. The Newbery committee's phone call woke Kaysandra Curtis at 9 AM. *The Watsons* had been named a Newbery Honor book. Although Curtis did not win the main prize, it was still a very great accomplishment to be a runner-up for the award. According to Curtis, Kaysandra has trouble waking up in the morning. Half asleep, she told the Newbery committee that her husband had gone to the library to write—and it's not absolutely clear what she made of the roar of cheering librarians in the background who heard this. Then her phone clicked because she had another call. The new caller was from the Coretta Scott King committee to say that *The Watsons* had won a Coretta Scott King honor. Again, it was not the main award, but these prize committees only give out a few honors each year. Receiving such an honor—especially with a first novel—is a very big deal.

By this time, Kaysandra Curtis was awake enough to talk, but evidently not awake enough to remember that she had left the Newbery committee on hold. Ten minutes later, she did remember, but they had hung up and called the Windsor Library. Christopher Paul Curtis found out about his awards when a librarian he knew came up and gave him a big hug. The author later said he knew "something was up, because while the librarians had always been very friendly they hadn't been that friendly!"[10]

Curtis's advance for *The Watsons* had been $4,000 and the book's sales had been good, but the honors would increase profits and get him paid invitations to give talks about his work. The awards would also help to fulfill one of Wendy Lamb's dreams for the book: that it would be included on the reading lists of materials approved by states for use in classrooms across the nation.

Perhaps the only disappointment concerning *The Watsons*—though Curtis is philosophical about it—has been the long-delayed efforts to adapt it into a movie. Soon after the book was published, Whoopi Goldberg bought film rights to the story and had even assembled a potential cast. She would play the grandmother. Yet over the years, Goldberg would be unable to find a studio willing to produce *The Watsons*, even with all the book's prizes, a great cast, and her own fame. She has since sold her rights to the book, but remains a friend of the Curtis family's.

4 *Bud, Not Buddy*

Curtis was still working at the warehouse unloading trucks, but he was also finishing his second book in 1997. Many people asked him if it would be hard to finish *Bud, Not Buddy*. Often the second book is the hardest for an author who has written a very successful first book. Nobody knows what to expect from first-time authors, but readers feel great anticipation as they await an author's second book. Suppose he or she can't do it again?

Curtis said it was sometimes scary, but usually noted that he had fun writing his first book and planned to keep having fun. Some writers complain that writing is hard. Curtis doesn't. Hard was the boredom of hanging a Buick door.

Writing was a delight. Curtis would sit in the library and laugh out loud when he was writing funny parts—earning him some odd looks from library patrons who didn't know who he was.

Curtis says his way of writing is inefficient, but it works for him. He usually doesn't know where a book is going when he starts writing it. *Bud, Not Buddy*, for instance, had started out as a story about the 1936 and 1937 labor strikes at the car factory. Then, in November 1996, three chapters into the story, he went to a family reunion and listened to stories about Grandfather Curtis and his Depression-era band. He'd found these stories boring when he was a kid, but now he wished he'd listened more carefully. For some time he thought the hero of his next book would be Grandfather Curtis at ten years old. But then he started hearing the voice of a ten-year-old orphan named Bud and somehow his grandfather became the sad, grumpy old man who appears in the final version of the book.

Often, when Curtis starts writing a book, he usually hears the characters' voices talking—particularly the voice of his main character. Some of his basketball buddies tease him, saying things like, "Let's hope no voices come into your head in here today!"[1] "Hearing voices" can, of course, be a sign of serious mental illness, but for Curtis they are a normal part of his writing process. He knows that he's hearing the voices of characters from his book and that they come from his imagination. Instead of outlining his books, he listens and the characters "speak" to him. Then he writes down what they say. He is so focused that he almost goes into a trance. This way of working often gives him more material than he can use, which is why it's inefficient. For instance, the manuscript for *Bud, Not Buddy* became so long that he and Wendy Lamb had to cut big sections from it. And the parts of his books don't necessarily get written in order. Curtis doesn't mind. He likes the surprise of what the characters will reveal later.

Bud

Although Kenny Watson knew that he could depend on his family, the main character in Curtis's second book, ten-year-old Bud, can not. When *Bud, Not Buddy* begins, readers learn that Bud's mother has been dead for four years and he never knew his father. He lives in a home for orphans during the Great Depression, a time when many children who had families became orphaned because those families were poor, homeless, hungry, and couldn't care for them.

During this time in history, there were very few jobs, and government programs like welfare were just beginning to gain support. Bud has learned to distrust adults. He lives by a series of life rules in which he describes how to survive among the homeless population in Flint, among them, his rule to sleep with an open jackknife. A particularly horrible experience at a foster home occurs when Bud is beaten, then locked in a shed full of "vampire" bats. Later, he escapes into the night.

Bud's life has been difficult for four years, but for the first six he had his mother's love. In Hooverville (a Depression-era encampment of homeless people), he meets a girl who says he carries his family inside him. He also carries a belief that his father was a musician. Bud has inherited a few of his mother's possessions, including some rocks that were written on and various fliers announcing the performances of Herman E. Calloway and the Dusky Devastators of the Depression. Bud decides that Calloway must be his father. Setting out to walk the 120 miles (193 kilometers) from Flint to Grand Rapids, he is rescued by a man with a red hat in a big black car—Lefty Lewis, obviously modeled after Curtis's other grandfather. Lewis delivers him to Calloway's club. Calloway wants no part of the boy or his story, but other members of the band volunteer to take care of him. When Bud meets the band's singer at dinner, he suddenly feels he has come home. After having been unable to cry for many years, he breaks down and sobs.

Bud does odd jobs for the band and begins to play a small saxophone, but his relationship with his "father" doesn't become any easier as they travel. Then one day Calloway tells Bud to hand him a small rock. (The man is too fat to bend over to get one himself.) Then, Calloway writes the initials of the place and the date on the rock before throwing it into the car's glove compartment. The rock is just like those that Bud inherited from his mother—rocks that he has cherished even though he didn't know what the writing on them meant. When he shows his rocks to Calloway, the truth is revealed: Calloway, always a difficult man, had pushed his only daughter too hard and she ran away with a drummer. But Calloway did love her, and he had brought the rocks to her when she was a girl, marked with the place and date of his performances. When Bud says his mother's name and shows a photograph of her, everyone realizes that Calloway is actually Bud's grandfather. Bud really has come home.

Research

Writing *Bud, Not Buddy* was a different experience for Curtis than working on *The Watsons Go to Birmingham—1963* had been. Although Curtis had to research Birmingham to write *The Watsons*, he was writing about a historical period that he remembered well. For *Bud, Not Buddy* he needed to understand a time in history before he was born. What was life like during the Great Depression? What did Hoovervilles actually look like? How did people talk back then? He read history books but he also read novels, magazines, and newspapers from the 1930s and watched old movies. For the Watson boys, an outhouse is something shocking. But for Bud, an indoor bathroom and hot running water are surprising—as is eating in a restaurant and sleeping in a bed with two sheets.

As with *The Watsons*, Curtis drew on family stories, most obviously those about his grandfathers. Small details also come into the story from his own life. For example, Calloway says that when he'd go on the road with his own band and ask his daughter what she wanted him to bring back for her, he would expect her to ask for a doll or a dress, but instead she wanted a rock. In fact, Curtis's daughter Cydney had [also] asked for a rock when he'd gone to Chicago on a trip. Also based on Curtis's experiences is Bud's reaction to being in a bedroom of his own for the first time. Curtis remembered sleeping alone in a room at his grandmother's house when he was little. Like Bud, Curtis was sure that those foolish grown-ups had left him there to attract every ghost around. But more than the Watson boys, Bud is a character created from Curtis's imagination.

Bud, Not Buddy contains the most opinionated statements about race that appear in Curtis's books. However, it is so subtle that readers could miss it. In Hooverville, Bud sees large numbers of people of all colors working together to survive. In the firelight, they appear in different shades of orange—not black, brown, or white. One white family stays apart from the group. Race matters to them, and their bigotry only serves to keep them away from the community that could help them. What the people in the camp have in common is far more important than their differences.

More Stars

Before *Bud, Not Buddy* was published, Curtis was already getting requests to speak at libraries and bookstores. He was finally able to give up those odd jobs he hated and devote himself full-time to writing. His $300 speaking fee eventually rose to $3,000. Now self-employed, he could also let his hair grow. Photographs of Curtis taken when he wrote *The Watsons* show a clean-shaven man with short hair and a suit. But once he could do what he wanted, he grew a cascade of Nubian locks and a big smile.

Reviewers liked *Bud, Not Buddy* as much as *The Watsons*. People loved Bud's life rules, and they loved Bud. However, Curtis has received some criticism for the way his books end. A few critics felt *Bud* ended a little too neatly; they would later say the same of *Bucking the Sarge*. Others had said that Curtis didn't leave enough time in *The Watsons* between the bombing and the end of the book. Yet even his critics say that at the end of Curtis's books, the reader does not begrudge the characters their happiness.

During the January following the publication of *Bud, Not Buddy*, the 2000 midwinter ALA meetings were held. Again, Curtis heard that his book might be considered for the Newbery Medal and Coretta Scott King Award. This did not make for a peaceful night at the Curtis household. That Monday morning he woke at three and couldn't get back to sleep. Nervously, he cleaned the whole house. Then Kaysandra Curtis took Cydney to school, leaving her husband with a telephone that—supposedly—would ring by about 9 AM with news of any awards. When the phone finally rang at 9:15, Curtis figured that it was his editor Wendy Lamb or someone calling with condolences. Instead it was a member of the Coretta Scott King committee saying that he'd won again—but this time, he won the main prize! At 9:32—"not that I was watching the clock or anything"—the Newbery committee called to tell him that he'd won the Newbery Medal. "[I]t was an overwhelming feeling," Curtis says. "You're numb."[2] Soon after Curtis received the calls, a press conference was held. Curtis's publishers held up a cell phone so he could hear the announcement made—and he burst out crying.

But the man who created Kenny, Byron, and Bud had to think of a more interesting way to tell his wife the news. By the time Kaysandra returned home, Curtis was draped on the couch reading a newspaper, very casually: "She said, 'No calls?'" and he said, "What if I won a Newbery Honor and a Coretta Scott King Honor, could I not do any housework for a year?" She took the bait. "You'd have to win both the Newbery Medal and the Coretta Scott King Award not to do housework for a year." He adds, "She's not a woman of her word—I'm still doing housework!"[3]

Winning the awards brought Curtis genuine fame and fortune. He was interviewed or profiled by *People, Time, USA Today,* and other magazines and newspapers that seldom pay attention to children's authors. He appeared on the *Today Show* and was invited to the White House for the annual Easter Egg roll by the Clintons and for two literacy programs run by Laura Bush.

In his Newbery acceptance speech, Curtis says that even if he wanted to, he couldn't become "too full of himself"[4] because the world won't let him. *Time* magazine published his weight (240 pounds [109 kg]). People mistook him for Walter Dean Myers, the famous African American children's writer who is Curtis's hero. And his daughter was still likely to answer the question, "What does your daddy do?" by saying, "Nothing."[5]

Still, to be told that his books are that good is a tremendous boost. As Luther says about his science fair medals in *Bucking the Sarge,* one prize might be "beginner's luck," but two says, "Oh, yeah, baby, this is the real deal."[6]

The combined sales of Curtis's first two books proved that sometimes a novelist can make money. Although a writer receives only about 5 or 10 percent of the price of each book sold, Curtis's books were selling hundreds of thousands of copies. Plus, he was making paid (and unpaid) appearances. Kaysandra left her nursing career to manage her husband's tours and speaking engagements. Soon other writers asked her to organize their tours, too. The Curtises were able to buy a five-bedroom house with an indoor pool, a basketball court, and a tennis court. Curtis has also been able to buy his dream car, a 1953 Buick Skylark. Although it was ironic for Curtis to purchase the very brand of vehicle that he used to assemble at a job he hated, the model was produced the year he was born, much earlier than the cars he had assembled.

The Curtises' son, Steven, was raised before his father had his literary successes. Steven finished six years in the navy to help pay for college and then considered going to law school. But Cydney, still a teenager, could have piano lessons, swimming lessons, and tennis lessons. The Curtises are also described as generous people by friends and family. A friend from college remembers that when they ate in restaurants, Curtis would always pay because he had a job. And Curtis likes to do things for children, too. Once, he hosted a small group of fourth graders and their teachers at his home. He answered their questions and autographed books, then played a joke on them, pretending to give a brilliant performance on the piano. His guests were terribly impressed until one of them was able to see that it was a player piano, and Curtis was only pretending to play it.

Curtis has always written in libraries—public libraries and the university library in Windsor. Like Bud, he's comfortable in them and even likes how they smell. In doing so, he reaffirms his parents' belief in the importance of reading. After Curtis began speaking at schools, teachers and librarians would tell him and Kaysandra about the trouble many children were having learning to read. Kaysandra then worked on a program that gives a literacy bag to each woman who has a baby in a Windsor hospital. It contained, among other things, a children's book, an informational pamphlet about the importance of reading, a T-shirt, and a library card for the child. The Curtises also raised money for the Windsor Public Library. For one fundraising event, Curtis offered to name a character in his next book after the highest bidder. In 2002, the Windsor Public Library opened the Kaysandra and Christopher Paul Curtis Children's Learning Center.

Bud, Not Buddy even helped Curtis finish his college degree. He had continued taking courses, but couldn't do the French exam to complete his last credits. When the chancellor of the University of

Michigan invited him to give a talk and discovered that Curtis was nearly a graduate, he awarded him his degree.

Curtis's travels became international when, in 2002, he went with illustrator Ashley Bryan to Kenya and other African countries to speak to children and visit schools. He saw a great deal of poverty, yet the conditions didn't depress him. Instead he found himself cheered by the children's courage. Although they were very poor, they cared so much about learning and could speak several languages. Curtis now tries to make a trip to Africa every year. He goes "to 'reconnect' with his roots and soothe his soul,"[7] as well as to help people with donations and gifts.

5 *Bucking the Sarge*

Curtis's success caused him one serious problem: his speaking engagements and charity work began to get in the way of his disciplined writing schedule. Time started to get away from him and five years went by between the publication of *Bud, Not Buddy* and *Bucking the Sarge* (2004), his first book for young adults. The book had originally been scheduled for publication in 2002. However, when Curtis realized he didn't know where the manuscript was going, he knew that he had to extend his deadline. With only three-quarters of the book finished, he told his editor "my daughter ate my disc,"[1] like a child who makes excuses for unfinished homework.

Writer Jerry Spinelli had warned Curtis that after winning the Newbery, he wouldn't be able to write for a year. There would be too many distractions, too many tours. In one interview, Curtis blamed his new big screen TV for his unfinished book. But what really happened is that he lost his discipline. Although he loves writing, he'd always treated it as a serious job, writing at the same time each day. After winning the Newbery and Coretta Scott King awards, he got careless. He's a procrastinator, says his editor, so he needed that strict schedule to keep him going. "[I]t's sort of like doing athletics," Curtis says. "You get into shape, you get a rhythm. Then something disrupts you and the longer you stay away, the harder it is to get back into it."[2]

In some ways writing about a fifteen-year-old was easier than writing about a ten-year-old, because the older youth is more knowledgeable and has a larger vocabulary. But Curtis found himself doubting if he could write a novel about a contemporary teen. He would soon conclude that he prefers writing historical novels to writing contemporary ones.

In between *Bud* and the *Sarge*, Curtis published introductions to new editions of two classic novels. One was to *The Prince and the Pauper* (2003) by

Mark Twain (1835–1910), one of his favorite writers. The story is about a prince and a poor boy who look identical and decide to pretend to be each other. Curtis says it was one of the first novels for young people that blended the humor of *Alice in Wonderland* (1865) with a serious message. Before *Alice*, he says, literature for children had been preachy and moralistic. In *The Prince and the Pauper*, each boy learns about the injustice of having his worth determined by fate, such as what family a person is born into. It is, Curtis says, something people have yet to learn. For example, in 1997, people around the world mourned the death of Great Britain's Princess Diana but just three years earlier, the murders of more than 800,000 Rwandans in Africa had scarcely been noticed in the same way.

Writing the foreword to *Uncle Tom's Cabin* (2002) by Harriet Beecher Stowe (1811–1896) was more complicated. Although the novel, first published before the Civil War (1861–1865), was an exposé of the horrors of slavery, it has since been criticized for its racist portrayal of blacks. Yet, says Curtis, writing the antislavery novel in the 1850s was a revolutionary act for the risks Stowe took and the outrage that she was willing to cause among proslavery forces. It is a book that is still worth reading 150 years after its publication, Curtis concludes, for what she revealed about that era.

Writing the *Sarge*

Years ago, when he was still living in Flint, Michigan, Curtis lived next door to a group home—a sheltered residence for adults who can't live by themselves. The homeowner's son, who was probably in his late teens or early twenties, but looked younger, had "a lot of responsibility."[3] The homeowner became "the Sarge" and her son became the would-be philosopher Luther T. Farrell, Curtis's first main character who could not depend on his family or memories of his family to support him.

Curtis has said, "Everything is about families. Human beings are fragile and if you don't get the support and encouragement that comes in a family you're going to have trouble growing and becoming a strong person."[4] Luther is the exception who tests that rule. He never knew his father, and he never received any tenderness or love from his mother because she had none to give. Carol Farrell, Luther's mother, tells Luther that when she was a student-teacher in a private school in New York City, she discovered that some of her students had real paintings by Pablo Picasso (1881–1973) hanging in their apartments. Their tuition cost more than she earned in an entire year. As she walked up the stairs to her fifth-floor apartment and saw her "black velvet painting of Martin Luther King, Jr. and John Fitzgerald Kennedy walking hand in hand with Jesus," she asked herself "What's wrong with this picture?"[5] She rejects the idealism and hope of the painting and instead decides to "milk the system for everything it's worth."[6]

She works double shifts at the Buick plant and creates what Luther considers a vicious and immoral empire. In this empire, she cheats neighbors with high-interest loans and slum housing, not to mention overcharging government agencies for goods and services she fails to provide at group homes like the one Luther runs. She destroys everything human in herself to beat a system that would otherwise have kept her and her family poor. Chester X. Stockard, a resident of the group home, endears himself to Luther by calling the Sarge a "lost-soul vampire."[7] At fifteen, Luther is not worried about the monsters that Kenny or Bud fear; he is concerned about the monster that his mother has become. Most of all, he does not intend to become one, too.

Some kids with terrible backgrounds mysteriously turn out OK, and Luther is one of them. He's a survivor. But Luther is also unhappy, and Chester can see that he is at risk: sometimes he speaks like his mother without meaning to. He is incapable of running his mother's "empire"[8] and she is not about to let her son fulfill his fantasy of becoming America's best-known philosopher. Chester wants them to escape to a little town in Florida where his family resides. Luther says no—until he wins the science fair with a project on the dangers of illegal lead-based paint. It's the sort of paint that Sarge has been using on her building for years. Luther's project is so convincing that the city government vows to crack down on the use of lead paint and punish the people who have used it. That's going to include his mother. After the Sarge gives him four days to vacate the premises, Luther collects the money the Sarge owes him, gets revenge on the Sarge's sidekick, undoes a little of Sarge's evil, and escapes with Chester.

As reviewers enthusiastically noted, *Bucking the Sarge* is a story of a kid who seems to have everything that many people think they want. Best friend Sparky does appreciate that Luther had to change the diapers on grown men when he was in the third grade. That might not have been fun, but Luther eventually ended up with an expensive vehicle, credit cards with no limits, and—supposedly—an education fund worth thousands of dollars. However, Luther knows that his mother's wealth was acquired at the cost of other people's suffering.

Critics disagreed about whether the Sarge is "two-dimensional" or the "novel's juiciest character,"[9] but noted that they were delighted to see the philosophical and loving Luther get his revenge. The Sarge says Luther's disapproval of her practices means he is an easy mark. The reader knows he's not. He is "a boy who needs to get out of the family he's in and go to some different kind of family."[10]

6 The Stories Inside Us

After his difficulties finishing *Bucking the Sarge,* Curtis became more regimented about his work schedule. He tried not to do more than two appearances at schools per month. But he also learned to give himself some leeway. Years ago, he'd found that about three hours of writing at a time was his limit. Today, as a more experienced writer, he found that sometimes three hours feels like "forever" and sometimes he can write for "eight or nine hours and still be fresh with it."[1]

Other Curtis books are scheduled. One upcoming title is *Elijah of Buxton*, a book about the Underground Railroad in the early 1860s in Buxton, Canada. Until now, Curtis has said *The*

Watsons is his favorite, but he says *Elijah* is on its way to being his new favorite.

When people ask Curtis what he doesn't like about writing, he has trouble thinking of anything. He sometimes says that he doesn't like letting go of his characters at the end of a book because he misses them. He has even talked of possibly doing a sequel to *Bud, Not Buddy*. Even after years of working jobs he hated, he can still scarcely believe that people will pay him money to write. Nevertheless, he would keep writing even if he couldn't make a living from it. In fact, he says he can't imagine anything that would stop him from writing—"maybe a blow to the head"—because if he couldn't write, he would feel "lost." "Writing," says Curtis, "is a way of thinking, a kind of way of discovering things."[2] It is calming. He loves that he can use his imagination to create people and to combine bits of stories he's heard. He loves that a writer can control everything that happens in the world of story—which, he says, "ain't something that's going to happen very often in real life!"[3] Sending each book out to be published, however, is harder. It turns him into a "bundle of nervous, overprotective, paranoid twitches,"[4] and so, he says, he is glad to have an editor he trusts, who he knows will treat his work gently.

When people ask Curtis how to become writers, he explains that they need to write every single day. Keep a daily journal. Listen. Read. Have fun. Ignore all the rules (after you learn them) and develop your own style. It is, he says, much like "learning a second language or playing a sport or mastering a musical instrument: the more you do it, the better you become."[5]

Curtis talks about taking "dictation" from his characters, which might make the writing process sound easy or magical or both. He says it's not either of those things. It's work. Writing also takes time. It took Curtis until he was forty to write a book he liked. Some people manage to do it at a younger age. Curtis says people should try: "I do believe we all have stories brewing inside of us, that it just takes the right amount of maturity, skill, dedication, and luck to get them down into a published book."[6]

Additionally, he would have his readers try to play a musical instrument or take up painting. As much as he loves playing basketball, he says too many African American children dream of sports as the only way to improve their lives, but very few make it. As a result, they're left only knowing how to dribble a ball. He suggests that it is better to practice to be a writer, a musician, or an artist.

The Truth

Early in *Bucking the Sarge,* Luther says, "Sometimes you don't know the true story until you've lived it. I've lived it. And believe me, some of the time the truth ain't pretty."[7] Curtis writes about ugly truths—violence, racism, poverty, and the exploitation of people—yet he writes about them in a way that makes us understand them better. Instead of wanting only to turn away in horror or despair, Curtis's readers want to learn more. The humor helps as does Curtis's inclusion of loving truths, like when a family of strangers helps Bud get breakfast at a rescue mission. Curtis shows the reader a complex world, yet his books aren't hard to read. He manages to sneak up on his readers in ways similar to that of famous writer Mark Twain. Although Twain often engaged his readers with humor and wit, he was also known to "sucker-punch," surprising them and knocking them flat with something they didn't see coming.

A trademark Curtis talent is putting more in his books than the narrator can understand and then leaving the reader to figure things out—or not. In *Bucking the Sarge,* a family that has been evicted leaves empty cans from cat food in their trash, but there's no other evidence of the family's pet. Luther guesses that they kept the cat's litter box as clean as they kept the rest of the house, but it is up to readers to realize that the family was eating the cat food themselves. In *The Watsons Go to Birmingham—1963*, Kenny never interprets the real meaning of the whirlpool. Curtis explains that the "Wool Pooh" is Kenny's way of trying to protect himself from something too frightening to bear, as well as a result of too little oxygen to his brain while nearly drowning. Curtis says that the way Kenny and Joella appear to each other is an example of his use of magical realism, a technique also employed by some South American writers. Rather than the magic of wizards' spells, it is a kind of magic that appears in everyday life. In *The Watsons*, the power of family love is what is magical.

Many children's authors make sure that every word and idea is accessible to the reader. Curtis is happy to allow readers to comprehend most of the symbolism and metaphor in his books or, in some cases, to figure it out later. After all, what ten-year-old always understands what his or her parents are talking about anyway? Adults in Curtis novels can be incomprehensible, boring, or wrong. That's reality. Curtis is also happy to add jokes that children will immediately understand. And Curtis also includes things that very few people will understand, like why Chester says the Brotherhood of Sleeping Car Porters were revolutionaries. Each of Curtis's books opens a door to a new time and to new truths. Each book ends with a renewed sense of hope. The ways people help one another become more powerful than the ways in which they harm one another. People find their families. Curtis intends to end all of his books with hope. He doesn't mean for readers to think life is easy, but he wants people to know dreams can come true. After all, his did.

Interview with Christopher Paul Curtis

The following is an excerpt of a 2003 interview of Christopher Paul Curtis by Dwight Blubaugh with Kristi Karns, Joe Latham, Amy Mestelle, and Amanda Weston, Blubaugh's fourth-grade students at Northwestern Elementary School in Eaton Rapids, Michigan. The complete interview is posted on the school's Web site, http://cnc.erps.k12.mi.us/~nwestern/blubaugh/authorarticle2.htm, as well as additional information about the school, its students, and Curtis.

NORTHWESTERN STUDENTS: Your two books, *The Watsons Go to Birmingham—1963* and *Bud, Not Buddy*, are both historical fiction, while your [most recent] book, *Bucking the Sarge*, is contemporary realistic fiction. Do you prefer to write about historical events or modern day events, and do you think you will continue writing about both?

CHRISTOPHER PAUL CURTIS: . . . I think historical is easier to write because you have so many resources you can go to to learn about a particular era or a particular time. When you're writing about stuff that's new or stuff that's going on now, contemporary things, it's not as much fun for me. I'm using my imagination as much, but it's good to go to the library and read books from an era or listen to music from that era or watch movies . . . And with historical fiction, I can take a lot of different things that have happened and put them in the book to make them more interesting, and the fact that they really did happen, I think, does make it more interesting.

NORTHWESTERN STUDENTS: What other genres might you write stories in?

CHRISTOPHER PAUL CURTIS: I don't know . . . This last book has taken me a long time to do. I don't know whether it's because it was a contemporary book that it's taken me longer to do or what it was, but I think my next couple will be historical. I don't like writing adventure too much. Well, I shouldn't say that. I think a good historical fiction has a lot of different genres in it. There's fiction, there's adventure, there's romance, there are a lot of different things that go into making a story more readable. But I can't think of any one particular genre that I will prefer to go to next.

NORTHWESTERN STUDENTS: Do you plan to continue writing strictly for children and young adult readers, or do you think you might ever write any books for adults?

CHRISTOPHER PAUL CURTIS: . . . When I write the books that I write now, I really don't think of them as books for children or young adult readers. I think of them really as stories, and I think a good story can be read by anybody . . . I don't think of myself really as a writer for children. Even though my narrators have been young people, I could easily write a book for adults . . . The writing of a book like [*Bucking the Sarge*] . . . is easier in some ways than a book for ten-year-olds because the older you get, you have a wider expanse of language that you can use . . .

NORTHWESTERN STUDENTS: You've mentioned that when you were growing up there was basically no black literature for children. What do you think of the current state of African American children's literature, and what changes have you seen in the last decade or so in this area of literature?

CHRISTOPHER PAUL CURTIS: Yeah, there weren't a lot of books that were for, by, or about black people when I was growing up, and sad to say, it's still the case in many ways. I am about the only male writer for young people in the 10-year-old middle readers. There aren't a lot of other African American male writers. There are some females, but Latino, African American, Native American are all underrepresented in literature . . .

NORTHWESTERN STUDENTS: You've mentioned that your favorite adult authors are Kurt Vonnegut, Toni Morrison, and Zora Neale Hurston. How much have these authors influenced you in your own writing?

CHRISTOPHER PAUL CURTIS: I don't think that they've influenced me a lot . . . I came to writing in a way that most writers don't come to it—writing is a profession that is very difficult.

It's something that you really have to work at and want. In the beginning, in particular, because there's a lot of rejection involved. There's a long period, an apprenticeship really, where you have to learn how to write, and learn how to tell a story, and I didn't go through that . . . So I don't think I was really influenced in any way by writers like that . . . I think it's kind of dangerous to use somebody as an influence . . . Nobody has lived the life I've lived. Even if there was someone who lived the exact same life I've lived, they would look at it in a different way . . . I couldn't tell a story about you as well as you could. And the fact that you could tell a story your own way and really without being influenced by someone, I think that's what makes writing special . . . I think that fresh writing is something that really comes from within you.

NORTHWESTERN STUDENTS: *The Watsons* and *Bud, Not Buddy* deal with issues of racial prejudice. Growing up in the 1950s and '60s in Flint you've mentioned that you were largely sheltered from racism. Both as a child and as an adult, what types of problems have you encountered with racism, and do you ever encounter racism still?

CHRISTOPHER PAUL CURTIS: Good question. Yeah, there's kind of a misconception about racism. A lot of times people think that it happened in the South only. But even in the '50s and '60s in Flint there was a lot of segregation. It wasn't enforced by law, but it was segregation nonetheless, and my parents were both involved in the Civil Rights movement. There were times we'd go out and picket stores or restaurants that wouldn't hire black people, so there was racism there. Yeah, you see racism all the time . . . when I was growing up, Canada had a reputation for not being racist, that there was not much racism in Canada. But once we've lived here, you get a kind of a different perspective. I think the country has changed because in the '60s and '70s there was a large influx of people from Africa and from the West Indies, and I think racism came to the fore. That was one of the surprises about moving to Windsor, that there's a lot of racism here . . .

NORTHWESTERN STUDENTS: Which of the characters from your books most reflect parts of your own personality?

CHRISTOPHER PAUL CURTIS: . . . I get this question a lot. So basically what people are asking, like with Byron and Kenny, they say which one are you, and the way I look at that question is, "Am I a juvenile delinquent, thug, and hoodlum, or am I a sweet, loving, kind, tender, sensitive, intelligent person?" The second one. No, all the characters are really composites. They're parts of me, they're parts of my brothers, my sisters, my parents. It's one of the really fun things about writing, that you don't have to have somebody there, you can create people. You can make them a certain way. It's something that you can combine the characters and make things. I think that in some ways I'm like Kenny and some ways I'm like Byron. Bud, I don't think I'm anything like. Bud was just a fellow who came to me, so I really don't think I'm much like Bud.

NORTHWESTERN STUDENTS: Other than living through the time period of *The Watsons*, what research did you need to do for that book and for *Bud, Not Buddy*?

CHRISTOPHER PAUL CURTIS: . . . For *The Watsons* I didn't have to do a lot of research, and there are two reasons for that really. Number one, I lived through the time, so I had an idea of what it was like. Number two, I was looking at it through the eyes of a ten-year-old boy . . . So you have to change their view a little bit. So I didn't have to do too much for that because I was a ten-year-old boy at that time, so I remember what kind of things I was thinking about. I did have to find out some things about the bombing of the church. I had to go back and—language changes from decade to decade, and they're pretty major changes. The way you speak is different from the way I spoke when I was your age, so kids talk in a different way . . . [For] *Bud, Not Buddy*, I had to do a lot more research. Originally it started out that I was going to do a book on the sit-down strike at the factory I worked in, but I didn't know anything about it, so I had to watch a lot of movies from the era to try to listen to how people spoke. I read a lot of books that were written in the '30s to get some kind of an idea of the kind of language, to catch the language and nail that. I listened to radio shows from the '30s. Just anything to try to expose myself to the '30s, to the kind of things that people would think. So, the older the book is, and the less knowledge you have about it, the more research you have to do if you want to make it realistic.

NORTHWESTERN STUDENTS: What do you like most about writing?

CHRISTOPHER PAUL CURTIS: . . . I like everything about writing. The only thing that I really don't like is the same thing that I'm sure that you don't like, which is editing and rewriting. You know, once something is done, leave it alone, it's done. But I love the creative process. I go to the library, I sit, I write, I use my imagination—that's a lot of fun. I create characters—that's a lot of fun. I get to travel a lot because I write. I love doing that. I meet a lot of interesting people . . . I hadn't traveled much before . . . now I've traveled all over the country. I live a great life.

NORTHWESTERN STUDENTS: What writing methods do you use when you write?

CHRISTOPHER PAUL CURTIS: What I do is I divide my writing into two very distinct parts. The first part, . . . I just sit down and I let it go. I don't think about the story. I just get information from whatever I want to write about that deals with the story, but I don't try to put it in the shape of a story. Then the next morning I usually get up very early, 5:00 or so, and I do editing and rewriting to try to make it part of the story . . .

NORTHWESTERN STUDENTS: About how much writing do you do per day?

CHRISTOPHER PAUL CURTIS: On a good day, I can probably do three hours of creative writing and then another couple hours of editing . . .

NORTHWESTERN STUDENTS: What do you want readers to come away from your books with? Do you start writing with a message in mind, or do the messages just work themselves into your books as you write?

CHRISTOPHER PAUL CURTIS: I think that, probably subconsciously, you'd have a message, but I think that's the kiss of death with a book when you start to read it and you can hear, "Here comes the message." I think that's terrible. What I want the readers to come away with most of all? I think it's very important that you have fun with the book. Reading is a very fun thing to do and if you have fun with the book, it makes you want to keep reading it . . .

NORTHWESTERN STUDENTS: Your life has radically changed since you won the Newbery Honor and the Coretta Scott King Honor for *The Watsons* in 1996. Then *Bud* won both the Newbery [Medal] and Coretta Scott King [Award] in 2000. What were the first things you did and thought when you learned that your books had won these important awards?

CHRISTOPHER PAUL CURTIS: With *Bud* winning the Newbery and the Coretta Scott King, you hope in your wildest dreams that these things will come true, but you never believe they will, and when it won, what really touched me and really got to me was they called and said that it had won the Newbery, and that was so thrilling to hear and I was on the speaker phone with librarians, and then one of the people from the publishing house called and said, "When they make the announcement to the public, we'll let you hear it. We'll hold the cell phone up so you can hear it." They called back about twenty minutes later and the person was sitting at the front of these librarians, and they said, "Here it is," and they held the cell phone up and started reading out who won, and when they said and the Newbery this year goes to *Bud, Not Buddy*, and then you could hear the people cheer. That really touched me . . .

NORTHWESTERN STUDENTS: What other noteworthy experiences have you had because of your literary successes?

CHRISTOPHER PAUL CURTIS: . . . So many wonderful things have happened. I've met a lot of people that I never would have had a chance to meet [such as] J. K. Rowling, Gary Paulsen, [and] Jacqueline Woodson. I was on the *Today Show* in Times Square . . . Scholastic made a poster of famous African Americans, with Martin Luther King and others . . .

NORTHWESTERN STUDENTS: Do you have any parting thoughts?

CHRISTOPHER PAUL CURTIS: . . . I'll just give the advice I give to writers all the time. There are three rules of writing, right? The first rule of writing is write every day. Writing is like anything else that you do, the more you do it, the better you get at it. The second rule of writing is to have fun with your writing. If you're having fun with something you do, you'll put a lot more into it, it's a lot more interesting. Make the writing fun. You can have fun with writing because when you write, you're in control of everything. Third rule—ignore all rules. Because you will learn your own way of writing. It's like the question you asked earlier about who influences me. You'll find your own way, and once you learn the basics—that doesn't mean ignore the rules of English or writing—there are certain things you have to do, but once you learn those things, ignore all rules, just have fun with it, go with it, and write it your own way . . .

© 2003 Dwight Blubaugh. Reprinted with permission.

Timeline

May 10, 1953 Christopher Paul Curtis is born in Flint, Michigan.
1971 Curtis graduates from high school.
1972 Curtis begins working at Fisher Body Plant Number One, a General Motors factory.
1977 Curtis meets Kaysandra Sookram at a basketball game in Ontario, Canada.
1978 Curtis's son, Steven, is born on May 6.
1985 Curtis quits his job at the Buick factory. The Curtises move to Windsor, Ontario, Canada.
1992 Curtis and his wife have a daughter and name her Cydney.
1993 Curtis receives the Avery Hopwood Prize for an essay about leaving the factory and begins writing full-time.

1994 Curtis submits *The Watsons Go to Birmingham—1963* to a contest at Delacorte.
1995 *The Watsons* is published.
1996 Curtis receives Newbery and Coretta Scott King honors for *The Watsons*.
1999 *Bud, Not Buddy* is published.
2000 *Bud, Not Buddy* receives the Newbery Medal and the Coretta Scott King Award.
2002 Curtis's introduction to *Uncle Tom's Cabin* is published. Curtis tours schools in Africa.
2003 Curtis publishes introduction to Mark Twain's *The Prince and the Pauper.*
2004 *Bucking the Sarge*, Curtis's first young adult novel, is published.

Selected Reviews from *School Library Journal*

Bud, Not Buddy
September 1999

Gr 4–7—When 10-year-old Bud Caldwell runs away from his new foster home, he realizes he has nowhere to go but to search for the father he has never known: a legendary jazz musician advertised on some old posters his deceased mother had kept. A friendly stranger picks him up on the road in the middle of the night and deposits him in Grand Rapids, MI, with Herman E. Calloway and his jazz band, but the man Bud was convinced was his father turns out to be old, cold, and cantankerous. Luckily, the band members are more welcoming; they take him in, put him to work, and begin to teach him to play an instrument. In a Victorian ending, Bud uses the rocks he has treasured from his childhood to prove his surprising relationship with Mr. Calloway. The lively humor contrasts with the grim details of the Depression-era setting and the particular difficulties faced by African Americans at that time. Bud is a plucky, engaging protagonist. Other characters are exaggerations: the good ones (the librarian and Pullman car porter who help him on his journey and the band members who embrace him) are totally open and supportive, while the villainous foster family finds particularly imaginative ways to torture their charge. However, readers will be so caught up in the adventure that they won't mind. Curtis has given a fresh, new look to a traditional orphan-finds-a-home story that would be a crackerjack read-aloud.

Bucking the Sarge
September 2004

Gr 8 Up—Luther's mother, "the Sarge," runs an empire of Flint, MI, slums and halfway houses, and has a loan-sharking business. At age fifteen, Luther manages one of her halfway houses, drives the residents around in a van with an illegal license, and readies the homes of evicted tenants for the Sarge's next desperate victims. In exchange, she puts his earnings in a college fund, threatens him into submission, and primes him to take over the business. All Luther wants to do is win the school science fair, think deep thoughts, find some action for the vintage condom in his wallet, and do something honest with his life. Curtis tells the teen's story with his usual combination of goofy humor, tongue-in-cheek corniness, and honest emotion. Accordingly, Luther narrates the absurd, embarrassing details of his life with both adult sensitivity and teen crassness. The dialogue between Luther and Sparky, his "womb to tomb" best friend, is at turns hilarious and touching. The Sarge herself is so convincingly sharp-tongued, shrewd, and despicable that she's the novel's juiciest character. The plot unfolds slowly at first, and teens may lose patience with Luther's tendency to feel sorry for himself. However, once his confidence begins to build, the story keeps a quickening pace with his character arc. His final revenge on the Sarge is so deftly constructed and the novel's resolution so satisfying that it makes up for the occasional lag in the lead-up. Any teen who's ever wanted to stick it to the man (or woman) will love this story.

The Watsons Go to Birmingham—1963
October 1995

Gr 5–8—In the only Newbery Honor book to make my list, the weighty issues and historical perspectives don't get in the way of a very funny family. Byron plays some awful tricks on his younger brother Kenny, but readers can't help but laugh at some of his less harmful teasing. He tells a convincing story to little sister Joey about how garbage trucks scoop up frozen Southern folks who don't dress warmly enough, and half-fools Kenny with his tall tale. While the boys supply many of the laughs, it's clear that they get their sense of humor from their dad. His gentle teasing and tongue-in-cheek exaggerations can be hilarious. Laughter and Tears Award: More than any other book on my list, the humor in *The Watsons* shifts to near tragedy and many thought-provoking developments. The serious stuff succeeds in part because readers grow so close to this family through the humor that comes earlier in the book.

Selected Reviews from *School Library Journal* reproduced with permission. Copyright © 1995, 1999, 2004, by Reed Business Information.

List of Selected Works

Bucking the Sarge. New York, NY: Delacorte Press, 2004.
Bud, Not Buddy. New York, NY: Delacorte Press, 1999.
Foreword to *Uncle Tom's Cabin*, by Harriet Beecher Stowe. New York, NY: Aladdin Paperbacks, 2002.
Introduction to *The Prince and the Pauper*, by Mark Twain. New York, NY: Modern Library Paperbacks, 2003.
The Watsons Go to Birmingham—1963. New York, NY: Delacorte Press, 1995.

List of Selected Awards

***Bud, Not Buddy* (1999)**

American Library Association (ALA) Best Book for Young Adults (2000)

American Library Association (ALA) Notable Children's Book (2000)

Coretta Scott King Award (2000)

International Reading Association Children's Book Award, Older Reader Category (2000)

Newbery Medal (2000)

New York Times Notable Book of the Year (1999)

Publishers Weekly Best Book (1999)

School Library Journal Best Book of the Year (1999)

***The Watsons Go to Birmingham—1963* (1995)**
American Library Association (ALA) Notable Children's Book (1996)
American Library Association (ALA) Top Ten Book (1996)
Coretta Scott King Honor Book (1996)
Newbery Honor (1996)

Glossary

antibodies Substances produced by the cells in the body that fight off bacteria or toxins.

begrudge To look upon with envy, resentment, or disapproval.

editor A person who corrects a manuscript and advises an author before the book is published.

enterprising Showing a willingness to take on new projects.

epilogue A short, concluding section to a literary work.

Great Depression The period of severe economic hardship experienced in the United States from 1929 to 1939 when a large percentage of Americans lost their jobs and homes.

historical fiction Stories where make-believe characters experience real-life events.

Hooverville An encampment, usually at the edge of a town, that sheltered individuals and families who became homeless during the Great Depression; named for President Herbert Hoover.

mainstay A chief support.

metaphor A figure of speech in which a term that ordinarily designates an object or idea is used in place of another to suggest a comparison or analogy.

paranoid Relating to a mental illness or state of mind characterized by extreme and irrational distrust of others.

procrastinator Someone who habitually delays doing things.

refuge A shelter from danger; a source of comfort in times of trouble.

setting Where and when a story takes place.

symbolism The representation of things by means or symbols.

theme A recurring idea in a story.

void An empty space.

For More Information

Web Sites

Due to the changing nature of Internet links, the Rosen Publishing Group, Inc., has developed an online list of Web sites related to the subject of this book. This site is updated regularly. Please use this link to access the list:

http://www.rosenlinks.com/lab/chpc

For Further Reading

Curtis, Christopher Paul. *Bucking the Sarge*. New York, NY: Wendy Lamb Books, 2004.

Curtis, Christopher Paul. *Bud, Not Buddy*. New York, NY: Delacorte Press, 1999.

Curtis, Christopher Paul. Foreword to *Uncle Tom's Cabin*, by Harriet Beecher Stowe. New York, NY: Aladdin Paperbacks, 2002.

Curtis, Christopher Paul. Introduction to *The Prince and the Pauper*, by Mark Twain. New York, NY: Modern Library Classics, 2003.

Curtis, Christopher Paul. *The Watsons Go to Birmingham—1963*. New York, NY: Delacorte Press, 1995.

Gaines, Ann G. *Christopher Paul Curtis* (Real-Life Reader Biography). Hockessin, DE: Mitchell Lane Publishers, 2005.

Bibliography

Allen, Jamie. "Author Follows Newbery Honor with New Novel for Young Readers." Cable Network News. September 21, 1999. Retrieved January 4, 2005 (http://www.cnn.com/books/news/9909/21/bud.not.buddy/index.html).

Baker, Deirdre. "A Very Good Year." *Toronto Star*, February 6, 2000.

Blubaugh, Dwight. "Celebrating One of Michigan's Most Prominent Authors: Christopher Paul Curtis Keeps Us Turning the Pages." Eaton Rapids Northwestern Elementary. Retrieved January 4, 2005 (http://www.erps.k12.mi.us/~nwestern/blubaugh/authorarticle2.htm).

Canton, Jeffrey. "Talking with Christopher Paul Curtis." *Book Links,* February–March 2001, pp. 32–35.

Curtis, Christopher Paul. "Autobiographical Statement." *Eighth Book of Junior Authors and Illustrators,* edited by Connie G. Rockman. New York, NY: H. W. Wilson Company, 2000.

Curtis, Christopher Paul. "Newbery Award Acceptance." *The Horn Book Magazine,* July–August 2000.

Curtis, Christopher Paul. "On *The Watsons Go to Birmingham—1963.*" *Alan Review,* Winter 1999.

Curtis, Christopher Paul. "Open a Door," *USA Weekend.* Retrieved January 4, 2005 (http://www.usaweekend.com/diffday/2000_articles/000917diffday.html).

Frazier, Kermit. "Alabama Bound." *New York Times Book Review,* November 12, 1995, p. 23.

Gaines, Ann G. *Christopher Paul Curtis* (Real-Life Reader Biography). Hockessin, DE: Mitchell Lane, 2005.

Goodnow, Cecelia. "'Sarge' Signals a New Discipline in Award Winner's Work." *Seattle Post-Intelligencer,* September 30, 2004.

Griffin, Amy. *Scholastic BookFiles: A Reading Guide to "The Watsons Go to Birmingham—1963."* New York, NY: Scholastic, 2003.

Habrich, John. "A Whole New Line." *Star Tribune*, December 15, 2002.

Hobbs, Valerie. "Flying Starts: Three Children's Novelists Talk About Their Fall '95 Debuts." *Publishers Weekly*, December 18, 1995.

Hodges, Michael H. "Author Goes from Factory to Fame." *Detroit News*, October 18, 2004.

Hodges, Michael H. "Children's Author Is Still a Kid at Heart." *Detroit News*, February 4, 2000.

Johnson, Nancy J., and Cyndi Giorgis. "2000 Newbery Medal Winner: A Conversation with Christopher Paul Curtis." *Reading Teacher*, December 2000–January 2001.

Lamb, Wendy, and Christopher Paul Curtis. "Author-Editor Dialogs: Christopher Paul Curtis and Wendy Lamb." Retrieved January 4, 2005 (http://www.cbcbooks.org/html/curtislamb.html).

Lamb, Wendy. "Christopher Paul Curtis." *Horn Book Magazine*, July–August 2000. Retrieved January 4, 2005 (http://www.hbook.com/article_curtisprofile.shtml).

Lesesne, Teri, and Christopher Paul Curtis. "Writing the Stories Brewing Inside of Us." *Teacher Librarian*, April 2000.

Lewis, Johanna. Review of *Bucking the Sarge*. *School Library Journal*, September 2004, pp. 202–203.

McCarthy, Cheryl Strizel. "Author Trades Factory Work for Top Honors." *Plain Dealer*, September 22, 2004.

Meriwether, Heath. "Nourish Children's Minds: Encourage Them to Read." *Detroit Free Press*, October 10, 1999.

Morgan, Peter E. "History for Our Children: An Interview with Christopher Paul Curtis." *Melus*, Summer 2002.

Morris, Ann. "Talk Writing with Winner of Newbery." *Austin American-Statesman*, April 2, 2000, p. K6.

National Public Radio. "Liane Hansen Interviews Christopher Paul Curtis." February 6, 2000.

New York Public Library Author Chats. "Christopher Paul Curtis." August 7, 2002. Retrieved January 4, 2005 (http://summerreading.nypl.org/read2002/chats/curtis_txt.html).

NothingButCurtis.com. Retrieved January 4, 2005 (http://christopherpaulcurtis.smartwriters.com/index.2ts?page=bio).

Random House. "Christopher Paul Curtis." Retrieved January 4, 2005 (http://www.randomhouse.com/features/christopherpaulcurtis/fag.htm).

Review of *Bucking the Sarge*. *The Horn Book Magazine*, September/October 2004, pp. 579–580.

Review of *Bucking the Sarge*. *Publishers Weekly*, July 29, 2004, pp. 162–163.

Review of *Bud, Not Buddy*. *Publishers Weekly*, August 9, 1999, pp. 352–353.

Scholastic Scope. "A Chat with Christopher Paul Curtis." April 4, 2000.

Smith, Russell, and Lorna Grisby. "His True Calling." *People*, April 17, 2000.

Sutton, Roger. Review of *Bud, Not Buddy*. *Horn Book Magazine*, November–December 1999, pp. 727–728.

Tarbox, Gwen A. "Christopher Paul Curtis." *St. James Guide to Young Adult Writers*, edited by Tom Pendergast and Sara Pendergast. Detroit, MI: St. James Press, 1999.

Telfer, D. J. "'No Mama, It's Bud, Not Buddy': Author Christopher Paul Curtis." *The Drive*, Issue 10. n.d. pp. 6–9.

Weeks, Linton. "A Winning Story: Curtis's Path to Newbery Medal." Retrieved January 4, 2005 (http://www.washingtonpost.com/ac2/wp-dyn/A41781-2000May10?language=printer).

Welsh, Dave. "Christopher Paul Curtis Goes to Powell's—2000." Retrieved January 4, 2005 (http://www.powells.com/authors/curtis.html).

Wergeland, Kari. "A Good Kid Overcomes His Bad Lot Winningly." Review of *Bucking the Sarge*. *Seattle Times*, September 11, 2004.

Winarski, Diana. "Christopher Paul Curtis: A Writer on Target." *Teaching PreK–8*, October 1999.

Source Notes

Introduction

1. Christopher Paul Curtis, "Authors Up-Close Program," TeachingBooks.net, retrieved November 30, 2004 (http://www.teachingbooks.net/spec_athr.cgi?name=Curtis%2c%20Christopher%20Paul).
2. Christopher Paul Curtis, "Autobiographical Statement," *Eighth Book of Junior Authors and Illustrators*, edited by Connie G. Rockman (New York, NY: H. W. Wilson Company, 2000).
3. Christopher Paul Curtis, interviewed by Dave Welsh, "Christopher Paul Curtis Goes to Powell's—2000," retrieved September 14, 2004 (http://www.powells.com/authors/curtis.html).

Chapter 1:

1. Ann Morris, "Talk Writing with the Winner of Newbery," *Austin American-Statesman*, April 2, 2000, p. K6.
2. Deirdre Baker, "A Very Good Year," *Toronto Star*, February 6, 2000.
3. Heath Meriwether, "Nourish Children's Minds: Encourage Them to Read," *Detroit Free Press*, October 10, 1999.
4. Christopher Paul Curtis, *Bucking the Sarge* (New York, NY: Random House, 2004), p. 50.
5. Heath Meriwether, "Nourish Children's Minds: Encourage Them to Read," *Detroit Free Press*, October 10, 1999.

Chapter 2:

1. Wendy Lamb. "Christopher Paul Curtis," *Horn Book Magazine*, July–August 2000, retrieved September 15, 2004 (http://www.hbook.com/article_curtisprofile.shtml).
2. Christopher Paul Curtis, "Autobiographical Statement," *Eighth Book of Junior Authors and Illustrators*, edited by Connie G. Rockman (New York, NY: H. W. Wilson Company, 2000).

Chapter 3:

1. Christopher Paul Curtis, essay quoted in Wendy Lamb, "Christopher Paul Curtis," *Horn Book Magazine*, July–August 2000, retrieved September 15, 2004 (http://www.hbook.com/article_curtisprofile.shtml).

2. Ibid.
3. NothingButCurtis.com. Retrieved September 15, 2004 (http://christopherpaulcurtis.smartwriters.com/index.2ts?page=bio).
4. Christopher Paul Curtis, "Newbery Award Acceptance," *Horn Book Magazine*, July–August 2000.
5. Christopher Paul Curtis, *The Watsons Go to Birmingham—1963* (New York, NY: Random House, 1995), p.11.
6. Ibid., p. 200.
7. Wendy Lamb, "Christopher Paul Curtis," *Horn Book Magazine*, July–August 2000, retrieved September 15, 2004 (http://www.hbook.com/article_curtisprofile.shtml).
8. Ibid.
9. Christopher Paul Curtis, "Newbery Award Acceptance," *Horn Book Magazine*, July–August 2000.
10. Teri Lesesne and Christopher Paul Curtis, "Writing the Stories Brewing Inside of Us," *Teacher Librarian*, April 2000.

Chapter 4:

1. Nancy J. Johnson and Cyndi Giorgis, "2000 Newbery Medal Winner: A Conversation with Christopher Paul Curtis," *Reading Teacher*, December 2000–January 2001.
2. Nancy J. Johnson and Cyndi Giorgis, "2000 Newbery Medal Winner: A Conversation with

Christopher Paul Curtis," *Reading Teacher*, December 2000–January 2001.
3. Ibid.
4. Ibid.
5. Christopher Paul Curtis, "Newbery Award Acceptance," *Horn Book Magazine*, July–August 2000.
6. Christopher Paul Curtis, *Bucking the Sarge* (New York, NY: Random House, 2004), p.164.
7. D. J. Telfer, "No Mama, It's Bud, Not Buddy," *The Drive*, Vol. 10, n.d.

Chapter 5:

1. Wendy Lamb and Christopher Paul Curtis, "Author-Editor Dialogs: Christopher Paul Curtis and Wendy Lamb," retrieved September 15, 2004 (http://cbcbooks.org/cbcmagazine/dialogues/christopher-wendy.html).
2. John Habrisch, "A Whole New Line," *Star Tribune*, December 15, 2002.
3. Cecelia Goodnow, "'Sarge' Signals a New Discipline in Award Winner's Work," *Seattle Post-Intelligencer*, September 30, 2004.
4. Christopher Paul Curtis, "Authors Up-Close Program," TeachingBooks.Net, retrieved November 30, 2004 (http://www.TeachingBooks.Net).
5. Christopher Paul Curtis, *Bucking the Sarge* (New York, NY: Random House, 2004), p. 100.
6. Ibid.
7. Ibid., p. 101.

8. Ibid., p. 146.
9. Johanna Lewis, review of *Bucking the Sarge*, by Christopher Paul Curtis, *School Library Journal*, September 2004.
10. Christopher Paul Curtis quoted in Random House, "*Bucking the Sarge* Q&A," Retrieved October 5, 2004 (http:/www.randomhouse.com/features/christopherpaulcurtis/fag.htm).

Chapter 6:

1. Christopher Paul Curtis, quoted in Random House, "Christopher Paul Curtis," retrieved October 5, 2004 (http:/www.randomhouse.com/features/christopherpaulcurtis/fag.htm).
2. Tim Podell (director), "Good Conversations: A Talk with Christopher Paul Curtis," (Scarborough, NY: Tim Podell Productions, 1995).
3. Christopher Paul Curtis, quoted in Random House, "Christopher Paul Curtis," retrieved October 5, 2004 (http:/www.randomhouse.com/features/christopherpaulcurtis/fag.htm).
4. Wendy Lamb and Christopher Paul Curtis, "Author-Editor Dialogs: Christopher Paul Curtis and Wendy Lamb," retrieved September 15, 2004 (http://www.cbcbooks.org/htlm/curtislamb.html).
5. Christopher Paul Curtis, "Autobiographical Statement," *Eighth Book of Junior Authors and Illustrators*, edited by Connie G. Rockman (New York, NY: H. W. Wilson Company, 2000).

6. Teri Lesesne and Christopher Paul Curtis, "Writing the Stories Brewing Inside of Us," *Teacher Librarian*, April 2000.
7. Christopher Paul Curtis, *Bucking the Sarge* (New York, NY: Random House, 2004), p. 12.

Index

C

E

F

G

About the Author

Judy Levin is a librarian at the Family School in New York City and a part-time author of children's books. She has long been interested in African American studies and the civil rights movement. Her most recent works include *A Timeline of the Abolitionist Movement* (2004).

Photo Credits

Cover © Time Life Pictures/Getty Images, Inc.; p. 2 © AP/Wide World Photos.

Designer: Tahara Anderson
Editor: Joann Jovinelly
Photo Researcher: Hillary Arnold